THE WONDER OF HORSES

THE WONDER OF HORSES

FOG CITY

PRESS

Published by Fog City Press,
a division of Weldon Owen Inc.
415 Jackson Street
San Francisco, CA 94111 USA

www.weldonowen.com

weldon**owen**
President, CEO Terry Newell
VP, Publisher Roger Shaw
Associate Publisher Mariah Bear
Project Editor Bridget Fitzgerald
Creative Director Kelly Booth
Art Director Meghan Hildebrand
Production Director Chris Hemesath
Associate Production Director Michelle Duggan
Consultant Erin O'Malley

Library of Congress Control Number on file with the publisher.

ISBN 13: 978-1-61628-788-7
ISBN 10: 1-61628-788-8

10 9 8 7 6

2017

Printed in China.

People and horses work and play
together all over the world.

We take care of horses. Horses
carry us on their strong backs
and help us with our work.

These beautiful animals have
become our very good friends.
Have you ever seen horses
like the ones in this book?

Baby horses are called foals. At first, foals like to stay close to their mothers. But soon they learn to run and play on their own.

Quarter Horse Foal

Quarter Horses

Fun Fact

Baby boy horses
are called colts.
Girls are fillies.

Welsh Mountain Foal

Norwegian Fjord Horse

Fun Fact
Some horses spend all of their time outside.

Quarter Horse

Assateague Ponies

Horses can have best friends—just like people do.

Fun Fact

Many famous racing horses are Thoroughbreds!

Thoroughbred Horse

Thoroughbred Horse

A father horse is called a stallion. A mother horse is called a mare. Mares make decisions for the herd.

Mustang Horse

Horses live all over the world. Some live in warm places . . .

Assateague Wild Horses

Fun Fact

A "bay" has a tan body and black mane and tail.

Arabian Horse

Fun Fact

Ponies are a smaller-sized breed of horses.

New Forest Pony

Haflinger Ponies

. . . and others live in cold places. In the winter, they grow thick, fluffy coats to keep them warm.

Andalusian Horse

Thoroughbred Horses

Alert ears and
a high tail show
that a horse
is happy.

Arabian Horse

Fun Fact
A horse is often looking where its ears are pointing.

Arabian Horse

Quarter Horse Foal

Horses come in lots of colors. A blaze is a white stripe on the face. White legs are called stockings.

Fun Fact

Horses lie down
only about 45
minutes each day.

American Paint Horse

Fun Fact

A white spot on a horse's face is called a star.

Horses on a Ranch

Quarter Horse

On ranches, working horses help cowboys move their cows.

23

Even though they are very large, most horses and ponies are gentle and friendly.

Exmoor Pony

Mustang Foal

Exmoor Ponies

Fun Fact

Horses are herbivores—they only eat plants.

Fun Fact

Horses can walk and run as soon as they are born.

Suffolk Punch Draft Hors

Suffolk Punch Draft Horses

Foals start out small, but they have lots of growing to do!

Fun Fact

Believe it or not,
horses can't burp!
But they can toot!

Shetland Pony

Shetland Pony

Ponies can live in the wild or on a farm, too.

Haflinger Pony

29

Connemara Pony

Show horses have their manes and tails braided for competitions.

Arabian Horse

Fun Fact

Ireland's climate makes it a great place for horses.

Irish Sport Horse

Fun Fact

Horses use their facial expressions to communicate.

Wild Welsh Mountain Ponies

Connemara Pony

Everywhere they go, from the mountains to the prairies, horses like to nibble on tasty grass.

33

Dartmoor Ponies

These horses are all saddled up.
Would you like to go for a ride?

Fun Fact
The Quarter Horse is the most popular breed.

Pinto Horse

Paint Filly

When horses play, they kick their legs high into the air.

Shetland Ponies

Fun Fact
There are more than 350 breeds of horses!

Arabian Horse

Fun Fact

Horses can gallop faster than 27 mph (44 kph)!

Arabian Horse

Arabian Horse

Horses love
to gallop on
their long,
graceful legs.

Arabian Horse

39

Fun Fact

Horses' eyes can see almost all the way around!

Falabella Ponies

Arabian Horses

A strong sense of smell and good eyesight help horses to learn about the world around them.

Clean water and
lots of grass to eat
help keep horses
and ponies healthy.

Wild Ponies

Welsh Mountain Pony Foal

Fun Fact
Horses drink ten gallons (38 liters) of water per day!

Falabella Ponies

Arabian Horse

Fun Fact
Horses can live to
be more than
30 years old!

Quarter Horses

Quarter Horse

Horses are happy to run and graze in their pastures . . .

45

Fun Fact

A yearling is a horse between one and two years old.

Quarter Horses

Thoroughbred Horse

. . . and grow up to be
friends with you!

Shetland Ponies

Key: t=top, b=bottom; DT=Dreamstime; iSP=iStockPhoto;
SS=Shutterstock.

2, 5 SS; 7, 9 iSP; 10 DT; 11 SS; 12t iSP; 12b DT; 13 SS; 14 iSP; 14, 15, 16, 17, 18, 19 SS; 20, 21 DT; 22 SS; 23t iSP; 23b DT; 24t DT; 24b iSP; 25 DT; 26, 27 SS; 28, 29t DT; 29b iSP; 30t iSP; 30b DT; 31, 32 SS; 33t DT; 33b, 34 SS; 35 DT; 36t iSP; 36b, 37, 38, 39 SS; 40 DT; 41 SS; 42, 43 DT; 44, 45, 46, 47 SS; 48 DT.